I0484834

Photography: The Complete Guide for Beginners

Learn How to Take Amazing Pictures and Freeze Life in a Moment

By Brian Pilts

Introduction

I want to thank you and congratulate you for downloading the book, *"Photography: The Complete Guide for Beginners. Learn how to take amazing pictures and freeze life in a moment"*.

Modern film photography is said to have been started way back in 1840s, the time when William Henry Fox Talbot combined paper, light, selected chemicals, as well as a wooden box to create photographic prints. Eventually, this innovation became refined to a greater extent and people found out new ways of doing photography. And that is when people started to discover the wonders of modern photography.

Sixteen decades after the discovery of photography, it is apparent that people now have improved the field. We have advanced technologies that help make photography a lot better and easier. There are the digital cameras that can capture images with great quality, and the computers loaded with photo-editing software that can help improve digital images.

While it is true that photography can be difficult sometimes, it does not necessarily mean that you can no longer do it. As a beginner, you will need this book to guide you through understanding photography. This book contains proven tips and techniques that will help you learn more about photography.

Thanks again for downloading this book. I hope you enjoy it!

Why You Should Read This Book

This book will help you learn how to take amazing shots. Basically, this book contains discussions on how to use your camera (most especially if you are still not that familiar with it), how you should properly compose your photographs, as well as how you can improve your digital images. Basically, this book has practically everything there is to know about photography. This book will be your best guide when it comes to learning photography.

Copyright

Disclaimer

The information provided in this book is designed to provide helpful information on the subjects discussed. This book is not meant to be used, nor should it be used, to diagnose or treat any medical condition. For diagnosis or treatment of any medical problem, consult your own physician. The publisher and author are not responsible for any specific health or allergy needs that may require medical supervision and are not liable for any damages or negative consequences from any treatment, action, application or preparation, to any person reading or following the information in this book. Any references included are provided for informational purposes only and do not constitute endorsement of any websites or other sources. Readers should be aware that any websites listed in this book may change.

Table of Contents

Chapter 1: Anatomy of a camera

When it comes to photography, your camera is your best friend. You can't do anything without your camera, of course. Therefore, it is important that you also know how to work with it. You must familiarize yourself with its features so that when you are already shooting, you would know what to do.

Common features of a camera

Camera features	Description
Auto power-off	As the name itself suggests, this feature allows you to automatically turn your camera off when not in use.
Auto-rotate	This one sets the camera's orientation when you take pictures. Also, when you preview your photos, they will automatically be displayed in the orientation that you selected.
Battery information	This shows you how much life your battery still has. There are also some camera models that show what type of battery is being used.
Date and time	This feature is for setting the date and the time in your camera. There is also an option is most cameras that let you put time stamp on your photos.
File naming	This one allows you to set the file naming pattern of the camera. By default, cameras save files in chronological order.
Grid	The grid guides you in composing your photo, which means that it is better to turn the grids on.
Language	Obviously, this feature lets you change the language setting of your camera, which by default is set in English.
LCD brightness and color	This one allows you to adjust the brightness and, in some models, the color of the LCD monitor.
Memory card format	This lets you format your memory card, which will

	erase all the files saved in there.
Revert to default settings	In case you have already done a lot of modifications in your camera settings and you can no longer figure out what went wrong, you can just go to this setting to reset everything.

Basic shooting and recording

Camera features	Description
Aspect ratio	Some cameras crop photos to a certain aspect ratio, like the high-definition aspect ratio of 16:9. But of course, this also means that some parts of the photo get cropped out.
Auto focus	This feature lets the camera adjust the focus automatically.
Auto ISO	This option allows the camera to automatically adjust the ISO level for proper exposure.
Dynamic range	This feature prevents overdoing the highlights that will in turn lose details in the shadows.
Image size and quality	The quality of the image matters a lot in photography. The higher the quality, the better. Also, the higher the quality, the higher the image size. This feature lets you choose the image size and quality (i.e. low, medium, and large).
Live view	This one allows you to specify how long the grid, exposure information, and autofocus modes will be displayed on the LCD.
Multiple exposure	This lets you take several photos with the same exposure.
No card	If this option is turned on, your camera will be able to take photos even without a memory card. Otherwise, it will prompt you to insert a card.
Noise reduction	You can select from these two types of noise

	reduction: long shutter speed and high ISO. The camera will automatically process the image according to the noise reduction setting that you have chosen.
Picture style	This one lets you set how the camera will process the image files, and you can choose from the following: Standard, Portrait, Landscape, Vivid, Neutral, and Monochrome.
Red-eye control	This one lets you reduce the red-eye effect when you are taking photographs with the flash on.
Review time	This feature lets you adjust how a photo will appear when you playback them.
Self-timer	This option lets you turn the self-timer on.

Chapter 2: Choosing the right camera settings

Some of the basic camera settings that you have to familiarize yourself with include the exposure, the focus, and the white balance and color temperature.

Exposure

Exposure refers to the amount of light that your camera's sensor can get, which means the higher the exposure, the brighter the photo. There are several factors that affect the exposure. These factors include aperture, shutter speed, and ISO.

- *Aperture* refers to the hole in an adjustable diaphragm set between the shutter and the lens where the light enters. Obviously, this means that if the aperture is big, more light will enter the camera, which leads to a higher exposure.

  Aperture is measured in numbers called the *f-stops*, which has the standard settings of f/1.4, f/2, f/2.8, f/4, f/5.6, f/8, f/11, f/16, and f/22. You have to be aware, however, that higher f-stop does not mean high aperture. In fact, it is actually the opposite—if the f-stop is high, the aperture is low. Otherwise, the aperture is high. Moreover, every f-stop lets in half as much light as the next f-stop, which means that your camera will get twice as much light as f/8 as it will at f/11.

- *Shutter speed* refers to how long the shutter will stay open. The longer the shutter stays open, the higher the exposure is because more light will enter the camera.

  Shutter speeds are measured in fractions of a second. For example, if you set the shutter speed at 1/8, it means that the shutter will stay open for one-eighth of a second. Though it may seem like a really small amount of time, a shutter speed like 1/8 is actually long enough already for the camera to produce a blurry image. The proper shutter speed to use is somewhere around 1/500. See the difference?

- *ISO rating* refers to the film's sensitivity to light and is also sometimes called the film speed. The most common ISO ratings are 100, 200, and 400. The higher the ISO, the more sensitive (or faster) the film is to the light. For instance, if the ISO rating is 100, you will need a bigger aperture and a slow shutter to properly shoot an image.

  Keep in mind, however, that higher ISO results to a grainy or noisy picture.

Automatic exposure

Most types of camera now have the autoexposure setting, which means that the camera automatically sets the exposure as it detects the light in the scene.

To let your camera automatically set the exposure, you just have to (1) make sure that the subject of the photo is framed within the monitor, (2) press the shutter button halfway and hold it until the camera sets the exposure, and (3) press the shutter all the way down to capture the image.

Semi-automatic exposure

Aside from the regular autoexposure mode of the camera, in which the camera sets both the aperture as well as the shutter speed, there is also the semi-automatic exposure, which basically gives you to freedom to control the exposure settings but still gives the benefits of the autoexposure mode at the same time.

Semi-automatic exposure comes in two options: the aperture-priority autoexposure and the shutter-priority autoexposure.

- *Aperture-priority autoexposure.* This semi-autoexposure mode allows you to adjust the aperture all by yourself. After setting the exposure by pressing the shutter button halfway (just like you do in autoexposure), the camera analyses the aperture that you have selected and then choose the proper shutter that will match the said aperture. Afterwards, you can now press the shutter button all the way down to take the photo.

- *Shutter-priority autoexposure.* Shutter-priority autoexposure mode, on the other hand, lets you choose the shutter speed yourself. As you press the shutter button halfway, the camera analyses the chosen shutter speed and then select the right aperture to match the shutter speed. After this, you can now press the shutter down to capture the image.

Focus

Focus refers to how sharp the image is. When the image is sharp, then it is in-focus. However, if it appears to be blurry, then it is unfocused. And of course, no one wants a blurry image (unless it is done on purpose), so your photo must be well-focused.

Focal length

Focal length essentially refers to how near or far the image sensor is from the lens. It is measured in millimeters and it specifies the angle of view of the lens as well as the size at which the subject will appear within the frame.

The focal length varies depending on the type of lens that your camera has, which comes in three types: normal, wide-angle, and telephoto lenses.

- *Normal lenses.* Normal lenses have a focal length of around 35 mm. In essence, normal lenses lie somewhere between the wide-angle and the telephoto lenses. The focal length of normal lenses is appropriate for the types of shots that most people take.

- *Wide-angle lenses.* Wide angle lenses have short focal lengths. This basically means that they have the visual effect of "pushing" the subject away from you, thus making the subject look smaller. As a result, you get to include more of the scene into the frame without having to move back.

- *Telephoto lenses.* Telephoto lenses, on the other hand, are lenses that have long focal lengths. These lenses bring the subject closer to you, and this means that it will look larger in the frame.

Autofocus

Just like how most cameras nowadays have the autoexposure mode, these cameras also have the autofocus feature, which means that your camera cam automatically set the focus after identifying the distance between the lens and the subject. And just like in the autoexposure mode, if you want your camera to automatically set the focus, you just have to (1) frame the subject properly, (2) press the shutter button halfway down and then hold it to let your camera identify and analyze the shooting scene and in turn set the focus, (3) press the button all the way down to take the photo after the camera has already set the focus.

Moreover, the autofocus mode of cameras falls in either of these two categories:

- *Single-spot autofocus.* The single-spot autofocus lets your camera identify the element that is located at the center of the frame and, based on this, sets the focus.

- *Multi-spot autofocus.* The multi-spot autofocus lets your camera identify the distance at various spots around the frame and then sets the focus in relation to the nearest element.

When you are on autofocus, it does not necessarily mean that you just let your camera do all the work for you. You should also be wary as to where you should place your subject within the frame as you lock in the focus. For example, if your camera uses the single-spot autofocus, then you have to place the subject right at the middle of the frame so that the focus will be set on it.

Manual focus

There are also some advanced cameras that let you do the focusing manually. Even though some camera models let you do the traditional mechanism of focusing, in which you will have to twist the lens barrel in order to set the focus, most types of camera actually involve the use of menu controls when choosing the distance at which you want your camera to focus.

Manual focusing is a lot helpful if you are trying to more than a few photos of a nonmoving thing. Since you can set the focus manually, you will no longer have to bother locking in the focus every time you shoot. You just have to make sure that you have properly estimated the distance between the subject and the camera when you are setting the manual-focus distance.

Moreover, if your camera is on manual focus mode and you are trying to do close-up shots, you have to measure the distance between the lens and the subject as accurate as possible. You may want to use a ruler to measure the distance actually. That is because if you are even an inch off in your estimate, you will most likely have a blurry image.

Depth of field

Depth of field, which is another important aspect of focus, refers to how much of the image will be in sharp focus. If the depth of field is larger, the area of sharp focus in turn will also be larger. The depth of field is controlled in part through the aperture setting.

If the image has short depth of field, only those things that are close to the subject will be properly focused. On the other hand, if you reduce the aperture, which in turn will increase the depth of field, there will be more elements put into focus. (Again, just in case you might have already forgotten this: the higher f-stop number, the smaller the aperture.)

If your camera does not have a zoom lens or aperture control, you can just edit the photo using a photo editing software. You can use the software's blur filters to imitate the effect of a short depth of field in your photo. Make sure, though, that you do not blur the subject. Also, make the effect look as natural as possible so that it won't appear as edited.

White balance and color temperature

White balance

Our eyes and our brain work together for different kinds of light, which is the reason why we see that a white object is white regardless whether we are looking at it under cloudy skies, or in the sunlight, or indoors with fluorescent light.

However, when it comes to photography, the lighting condition has a great effect on the color of the object. Unlike our eyes and brain, digital cameras are in need of help to understand the different types of lighting condition and to realize that a white object is white. That help is known as the white balance.

We can just set auto white balance and let the camera read the color temperature of the scene. Afterwards, the camera will select a setting from all the adjustments that are programmed to it. This is a lot helpful when the lighting condition in a scene is somewhat all of one type and a neutral or white subject that is prominent. However, there are some cases when you will have to set the white balance manually to render the most accurate color for the scene. You can choose from the different white balance settings, which include—but not limited to—incandescent, flash, fluorescent, sunny, and open shade.

Color temperature

Each light source has its own color temperature that differs from red to blue. For example, sunsets, tungsten bulbs, and candles emits light that are close to red, which in turn give pictures the warm look. On the other hand, blue skies give out the cool blue light.

If you set the white balance of your camera manually, you can select from several pre-set color temperatures that your camera has, such as Daylight, Tungsten, Cloudy, and Shade. You can also customize your own setting.

Color temperature is usually recorded in kelvin (the unit of absolute temperature.) Blue and other "cool" colors in general have color temperatures of more than 7000 K, whereas red and other "warm" colors have color temperatures of around 2000 K.

Chapter 3: Taking your best shot

Okay, enough of those technical details about photography. Let us now get into the real action: taking the photographs.

Photography isn't just about pressing the shutter button. It is more about how you compose your photo to make them look interesting, which leads us to our next topic: photo composition.

Photo composition refers to how you compose your photo (obviously) by positioning the subject within the frame. There isn't really the "best" way of composing photographs; it still depends on how you want the subject to be projected in the photo. The way you compose your photograph can have an effect on how the people will view it.

However, just because photo composition is still quite subjective, it does not necessarily mean that you can do whatever you want with your photo. While this may work at some point, it is still better that you follow these photo composition guidelines, most especially because you are still in the process of learning photography. Here are some of the helpful tips that you must keep in mind vis-à-vis photo composition:

Apply the rule of thirds

Rule of thirds is one of the most popular concepts in photography. If you have already been reading other photography books or if at least if you know something about photography, then it is most likely that you have already heard about rule of thirds. Basically, rule of thirds suggests that you must not put the subject of your photo right at the very center of the frame, or else it will look dull. For maximum impact and better composition, you must place the subject right where the lines of the grid intersect, as shown in the figure below:

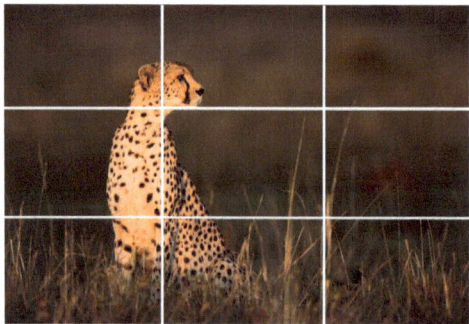

(Photo source: www.photovideoedu.com)

As you will notice, the tiger in the photo wasn't positioned at the centermost part of the frame. Rather it was placed right where the lines on the left intersect with each other. *That* is what the rule of thirds is all about. Also, this is when the grid feature (which we have talked about in Chapter 1) will be a lot helpful since it will guide you in positioning your subject properly within the frame.

Draw the viewer's eyes across the frame

It is also important that you lead the eyes of your viewers from one edge of the frame to another in order to add life to the photo. Don't make them stare only at one point of the image, or else it will look dull.

For instance, take a look at the photo below. As you may have noticed, your eyes are drawn from one edge of the image (body of the statue) to the other (the torch). Your eyes naturally follow the direction of the statue's arm, which is why the photographer took advantage of the statue's hand position to direct the eyes of the viewer from the body to the torch.

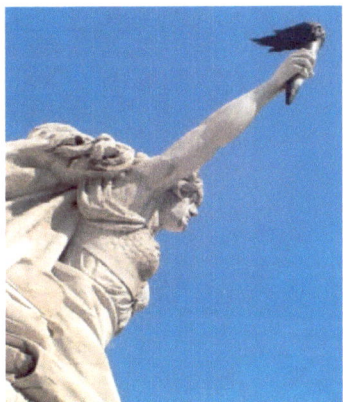

(Photo source: Digital Photography for Dummies)

Take pictures at unexpected angles

When you are taking photos, you don't necessarily have to stand right in front of the subject all the time and then just press the shutter button right there and then. You should also learn how to play with camera angles to add more dramatic effect as well as life to the image. If you take the photo at a flat angle of view, the image will also most likely fall flat and uninteresting. However, if you shoot from less obvious and unexpected angles, you will most likely get more interesting shots.

Take a look at the next page below for the example.

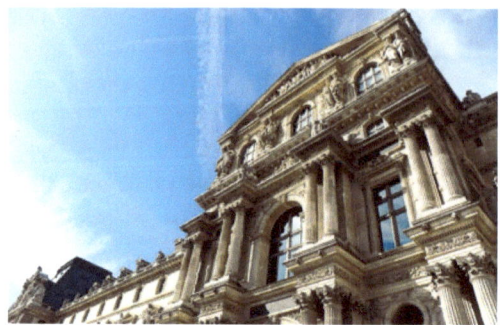

(Photo source: www.fodors.com)

If you will notice in the image above, the photographer took the photo of the building at a low angle to show the viewers that the building is tall. Had the photographer shot the photo at an eye-level angle, the subject won't appear as tall as it does with this angle.

Capture the personality of your subject

If you take a shot of someone sitting there and doing nothing but smile when you said "Say Cheese!" the shot will most likely be boring and not that interesting since the photograph itself doesn't say anything about the subject. If you really want to tell something about your subject through the photograph, then it is best if you will catch them doing things that best characterize them. For instance, if you want to show that your mom is a good cook, then you should take a photo of her cooking food. It is also better if you will be able to take candid shots as these shots will most likely show the natural expression of your subjects.

Reveal small details in your shot

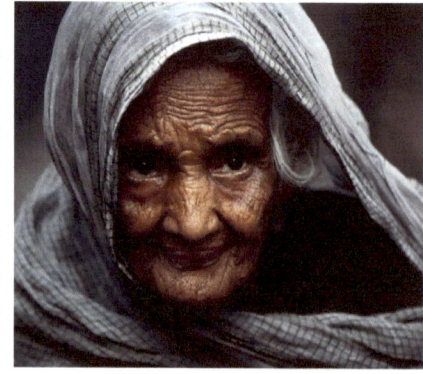

Usually, it is the close-up shots that are able to show more emotions and appear to be more interesting. These images reveal small details of the subject, which make it catchier. Look at the image at the right (Photo source: revolutionizingawareness.com):

As you can see, the image was shot with a close distance between the camera and the old woman. In this case, the wrinkles all around the face of the woman were clearly shown, which implies old age.

Pay attention to the background as well

The background is just as important as the subject. Before shooting, you must first consider the background. Do a quick scan of the surrounding and assess if the background is too busy to be distracting. Also, check if there is anything in the background that might be off-putting. For instance, if you are in a restaurant and there are lots of people behind your subject—of course there are, it's a public place—you can shoot at a different angle or position just so there won't be any "photobomber" in the frame. You may also want to take advantage of the depth of field, in which the sharp focus will only be on the subject and the rest of the background will be blurry.

Chapter 4: Improving your images

1. Always think about the resolution.

Resolution is an important aspect of a photograph. Photos are composed of several small squares known as the *pixels* (short term for picture element). Open an image in your computer or iPad and zoom in until you can no longer zoom in. Can you see the tiny squares that make up the entire photo? Those are what referred to as the pixels. Now, zoom out. The pixels look blended together, right?

Most cameras nowadays have various capture settings that offer a certain number of pixels. Of course, the higher the number of pixels, the higher the image quality. However, you first have to consider your purpose of using the image. If you are going to print it on a large paper, then you will need lots of pixels. On the other hand, if you are just going to upload it on Facebook or any other social media accounts, then you will need lesser number of pixels.

2. Minimize compression.

The most common file extension for images nowadays is the JPEG, which stands for Joint Photographic Experts Group. As an image gets saved, it undergoes the process of *JPEG compression*, in which it gets rid of some image data so that the file size will be relatively smaller. Of course, JPEG compression has an effect on the quality of the photo. The more data an image loses, the lower the quality will be.

Most cameras allow people to choose their desired JPEG settings: Best, Better and Good, or Fine and Normal.

3. Shoot at an unexpected angle.

As what we have talked about in Chapter 3, the angle can add an effect to the image. Instead of shooting at the usual angle, shoot the image at an unexpected angle to make it look more unique and appealing. Also, the angle can help you project the subject better, such as the example shown in the previous chapter.

4. Lessen the noise.

Some photos suffer from the problem known as *noise*, which makes the quality of the photo worse. Therefore, you must eliminate the noise as much as possible by (1) adding more light by either using the camera's flash or putting some more sources of light near the subject since it can help get rid of the noise, since it usually appears when the lighting is dim; and lowering the ISO value for this will increase the sensitivity of your camera to light, which in turn allows you to shoot photos even when the lighting is dim.

5. Do not use digital zoom.

Digital zoom, which is a software process that lets your camera enlarge an existing image and then crops the perimeter away, is a common feature in most camera models. In essence, you just get the same results as you would when you open an image in a photo editing software and crop that image. Moreover, digital zoom also does not have any effects on the depth of field, like a real zoom lens. Instead of using the digital zoom, just come near the subject so that you won't lose anything.

6. Press the shutter button properly.

This may seem quite silly to some, but it is one of the most important thing that you should always keep in mind when it comes to taking photographs. Improper pressing of the shutter button usually results to an out-of-focus or incorrectly exposed shot. Since most cameras nowadays offer auto exposure and autofocus features, exposing and focusing the image can be done easily. However, even though these features are pretty much automatic already, you still have to press the shutter button properly.

As what we have discussed in Chapter 2, in order to let your camera automatically set the focus and the exposure, you first have to press the shutter button halfway through and hold it there until the exposure and the focus are already set. Afterwards, press the shutter all the way down to take the photo.

7. Learn how to use photo editing software.

As a photographer, you will not only need your camera in order to make the best shots. You will also need photo editing software to enhance the overall quality of the photos that you have taken. You should not just automatically toss all the photos, especially if they do not look as good as you want them to.

With the help of the right photo editing software, you can retouch your photos and enhance their quality by correcting the color balance, brightening the underexposed photos, cropping out unnecessary and distracting elements that have been included in the shot, or even cover up some blemishes on the face of your subject. You can do practically anything with photo editing software, especially the high-end ones.

Since most photo editing programs out there are pretty expensive, there are some that are available for free. You can easily download them from the developer's site and they won't cost you a single buck. These programs can also be easy to use, as most of them require merely one click of the mouse button. However, these free programs may lack some of the helpful features that most paid programs have.

8. Read your camera's manual.

The manual is one of the most important things that come with a product. However, most people tend to neglect this and not even read it. So in case you have already forgotten, yes, your camera has a manual, too. I understand, manuals can sometimes be boring, but it is important that you read it once in a while. It does not mean that you should read it in one sitting or read it just like you read novels (of course that doesn't work that way!) but at lease use it as a guide that will help you familiarize yourself with your camera.

9. Practice.

As an old saying goes, "practice makes perfect." As a beginner, you can't expect to get the best results at the first try. It will take time and of course practice. All you have to do is to practice taking photographs, one step at a time. You don't need to do everything at one sitting. For instance, today you can explore the features and settings of your camera (don't be afraid to navigate; again, there is a manual); tomorrow you can practice how to set the exposure; after that, you can play with focusing.

It doesn't matter how long it takes you to get used to these things; what's more important is that you do your best and practice a lot. Again, you should not be frustrated if the photos you take are still not that good. Just practice again and again until you already know how to do things.

Bonus Chapter: DSLR vs. point-and-shoot

We have discussed in Chapter 1 the important features and settings of your camera that you should be familiar with. But if you have a point-and-shoot camera, you will most likely not see some of those features. On the other hand, if you are using a DSLR camera, you will understand what I was talking about in Chapter 1.

One of the most common photography-related questions that people ask is: "What is the difference between point-and-shoot and DSLR cameras?" Or: "Which one is better?"

From point-and-shoot to DSLR

It is undeniable that point-and-shoot cameras are a lot simpler and easier to use because, as the name itself implies, it is designed for just pointing the camera to the subject you want and then shoot it. And obviously, point-and-shoot cameras are lighter and smaller, which means that you can easily take it anywhere with you.

However, if you really want to take photography seriously, then probably it is about time that you let go of your old point-and-shoot camera and get yourself a DSLR, or *Digital Single Lens Reflex*. If you would compare a DSLR camera with a point-and-shoot one, you will notice that the former has so much more advanced features that the latter doesn't have. Also, DSLRs can capture photographs with better qualities as compared to point-and-shoots. Though they are generally a lot bigger and heavier than point-and-shoots, they are more capable when it comes to taking high-quality images since they are actually designed to have a better sensor, a set of controls, and a set of interchangeable lenses.

A lot of professional photographers out there would say that "it is not the camera that takes the photos but you." Some may even argue that the quality of the photos you take does not really depend on what camera you use but rather on how you use it, it will still be a bonus if you have a good camera with better features.

To convince you even more, here are some reasons DSLR cameras are generally better than point-and-shoots:

1. DSLR cameras can produce images with better qualities. Typically, the sensor of a DSLR camera is bigger than that of the point-and-shoots, which means that it can capture photos with less noise and, of course, better quality.

2. DSLR cameras have better sensitivity to light, which means that they are better to use even in very dim settings. With a DSLR, you can easily capture better photographs even if it's dark than you would with a point-and-shoot.

3. DSLR cameras have better focus as well as shutter speeds. Generally, DSLRs can focus fast and capture multiple images per second (in fact, high-end DSLRs can capture up to 10 shots per second). Therefore, DSLRs are more appropriate if you

usually take photos of moving subjects, such as an athlete in a sport event or a moving child.

4. DSLR cameras have more flexible controls. Essentially, point-and-shoot cameras are created for simplicity and convenience. DSLRs, on the other hand, are designed to offer more advanced features, which is why they have more buttons and controls.

5. DSLR cameras are usually more durable than most point-and-shoots. DSLRs come with solid construction so they will last longer than the typical point-and-shoot cameras. While there are some parts of a DSLR that are made of plastic, professional ones are made of magnesium alloy, which makes the camera more durable.

Conclusion

Thank you again for downloading this book.

I hope that this book was able to give you useful and comprehensive discussion about photography. I also hope that you find this book interesting and easy to understand as this book was written for beginners. Also, I hope that this book was able to inspire you to pursue photography, no matter how complicated it may seem.

After reading this book, the next step for you is to apply all the things that you learned from this book in real life. Of course, it is not enough that you merely read this book and then do nothing afterwards. Simply knowing the things that we have discussed in this book is not enough. You already know how to compose photos as we have talked about it in Chapter 3? Then might as well bring your camera with you and practice photo composition. Don't worry if you forget some things that discussed in this book; you can always go back and review what you have forgotten. It doesn't matter how long it takes you to fully comprehend everything; the most important thing is that you learn them and that you apply what you learn in actual life.

But more than anything else, it is just as important that you are enjoying what you are doing. Have fun pressing that shutter button. Also, do not expect the best output on your first try. Don't get frustrated when you can't get the result that you want. Just keep on taking shots after shots until you can already get the best results that you desire.

So I guess that's it. I hope you enjoyed this book as much as I enjoyed writing it. Thank you again and good luck!

One Last Thing…

If you enjoyed this book or found it useful I'd be very grateful if you'd post a short review on Amazon. Your support really does make a difference and I read all the reviews personally so I can get your feedback and make this book even better.

If you'd like to leave a review then all you need to do is click the review link on this book's page…

Thank you so much.

www.ingramcontent.com/pod-product-compliance
Lightning Source LLC
Chambersburg PA
CBHW041622180526
45159CB00002BC/971